IMAGES
of America

WILMINGTON

The Whitefield Elm on Middlesex Avenue, c. 1898. According to local legend the tree was named for the Reverend George Whitefield, an English divine who traveled around colonial New England preaching God's word. It is said that because of his unorthodox views he was denied the use of the pulpit in the local meetinghouse and in response chose to preach from beneath this tree to whomever would hear him. It is the view shown in this photograph that local historian Arthur Thomas Bond chose as the basis for the town of Wilmington's official seal in 1899. Most of the features and detail in the photograph, such as the Squire Samuel Eames House on the left, can be found in the original wax impressions of the seal. The tree was purposely felled in 1900 because of age and disease.

IMAGES
of America

WILMINGTON

Paul L. Chalifour

ARCADIA

First published 1998
Copyright © Paul L. Chalifour, 1998

ISBN 0-7524-0857-7

Published by Arcadia Publishing,
an imprint of the Chalford Publishing Corporation,
One Washington Center, Dover, New Hampshire 03820.
Printed in Great Britain

Library of Congress Cataloging-in-Publication Data applied for

Contents

Acknowledgments

I would like to thank the following people and organizations whose assistance and expertise made this book of Wilmington, Massachusetts, possible: Chairperson Carolyn Harris, Ann Humphrey Berghaus, Dorothy Lafionatis, Jim Murray, Kathy Reynolds, Jean Rowe, and Frank West of the Wilmington Historical Commission; Assistant Town Clerk Carolyn Kenney; Library Director Tina Stewart, Reference Librarian Laurel Toole, and the staff of the Wilmington Memorial Library; Town Manager Michael Caira and the Board of Selectmen; Superintendent Bob Palmer of the Department of Public Works; Chief Bobby Stewart of the Wilmington Police Department; Terry McKenna, Bob Varey, and Bob Woods of the Wilmington Fire Department; Rob Antico, Mike Ferrara, Gerry Lawrenson, and Cliff Preble of the Wilmington Water Department; and Fr. Rickard O'Donovan of St. Dorothy's Church.

I also wish to thank Mark Costain, Les and Maureen Chisholm, Jim and Diane Cleary, Francis Crispo, Ethel Fitzgerald, Andrea Houser, Maryann Langone, Norinne Markey, Gerry O'Reilly, and Ken Warren.

Special thanks and gratitude go out to the following people: Town Clerk Kay Scanlon, for allowing me to delve into both the photographic archives of the town and the scrapbook of her father, Nifty Hoban; Adele Passmore, for her time, historical knowledge, and dozens of photographs; Bill Dayton, for relating to me his remembrances of yesteryear and letting me peruse his many scrapbooks; Ruth Childs, for her legwork in gathering and passing along to me information about the Sheldon family; Captain Larz Neilson, Stu Neilson, and Frank Amato of the *Town Crier* for their many personal photographs and their genuine interest in the history of Wilmington; Rapid Reproduction of Wilmington and Andover Photo for accommodating my copying needs; and my parents, Marilyn and Leon Chalifour, for editing and running errands.

Lastly, I wish to thank my wife, Debbie, who has let me put many projects and activities on hold over the past year so I could concentrate on this project. Her love and support will always be appreciated.

Introduction

The town of Wilmington, Massachusetts (named to honor Englishman Spencer Compton, the first Earl of Wilmington and a member of the Privy Council of King George II), finds its origins in the earliest history of the Massachusetts Bay Colony. In 1640 the town of Charlestown encompassed many thousands of acres of land which stretched north, away from Boston into the Merrimack River Valley. Political and religious control over and within such a vast area was often difficult to maintain. It was inevitable that the area would soon be divided up into smaller townships. This first took place in 1642 when Charlestown Village, the northern section of Charlestown, became the town of Woburn. Two years later the western edge of Lynn, called Lynn Fields, became the town of Reading. It was the north part of Woburn (known as the "Land of Goshen"), the west part of Reading, land still claimed by Charlestown (known as the "Land of Nod"), and about 600 acres of East Billerica that formed the town of Wilmington.

It is difficult to be infallible in naming the first white settler in what is now Wilmington, as there are several legitimate claimants. About 1665 Will Butter (whose family name later became Butters), a former indentured servant, traveled over Wood Hill to the "Boggy End" of Woburn and settled on what is now Mill Road near Chestnut Street. In that same year Sergeant Abraham Jaquith settled on Aldrich Road, just south of Lubber's Brook across from present-day Forest Street. Richard Harnden is said to have built his house on High Street in the late 1660s, and Roger Buck's house at the corner of Wildwood and Woburn Streets dates from 1671. Whoever the first settler was and the date he arrived remains a subject for debate. One fact is clear, however—by 1720 enough people had moved into these outlying sections of Woburn, Reading, and Charlestown that the issue of a separate town and place of worship became a serious topic. In 1729 two petitions to the General Court, sent by prominent citizens John Harnden, Samuel Eames, Daniel Pierce, Benjamin Harnden, and Samuel Walker, asked to form a separate town but were rebuffed. The next year a favorable ruling allowed the town's establishment. A condition attached to this ruling was that the town would build a meetinghouse and obtain a worthy minister within three years. "An Act for erecting the northeasterly part of Woburn and the westerly part of Reading into a township by the name of Wilmington . . ." begins the document of incorporation allowed by the General Court of Massachusetts Bay on September 25, 1730. The first meetinghouse was built in 1732 and the church was organized on October 24, 1733, with the Reverend James Varney serving as its first minister. In 1737 the General Court granted a request from Billerica citizens Abraham Jaquith (son of Sergeant Jaquith), John Beard, Ebenezar Beard, Jacob Beard, Peter Cornell, Jonathan Baldwin, and Richard Hopkins asking to join their farms to Wilmington. These families were accommodated in order to lessen the distance they would need to travel to a place of worship. It was with this additional land that Wilmington took on its current size and shape.

For many years following its incorporation Wilmington enjoyed a peaceful existence as a rural farming community. In March of 1775 increasing tension with the British Crown forced its inhabitants to call on every able-bodied man age sixteen to sixty to gather arms and ammunition in preparation to defend their liberties. A month later three companies of minutemen commanded by Captain Cadwallader Ford, Captain Timothy Walker, and Captain John Harnden marched on the alarm of April 19 to engage British troops at Lexington and Concord. By the time the Revolutionary War ended over 250 of Wilmington's citizens had taken up arms and fought for America's independence from Britain.

In the early part of the nineteenth century Wilmington continued to develop as both an agricultural community and a crossroads of early transportation systems. It was during this time that Wilmington became known as "Hoptown." Nearly every farm and home was engaged in the growing of hops, a necessary ingredient in the production of beer. Hop growing was so important in town that one resident, Squire William Blanchard Jr., became the official "state inspector" of hops. In 1793 the Middlesex Canal Corporation was formed. This artificial waterway built by men with picks and shovels opened in 1803 and connected the Merrimack River with Charlestown. The canal greatly facilitated the transportation of textiles, agricultural products, and people, but ironically its success led to its own demise. In its final years of operation the canal's boats were relegated to carrying the building materials for the new railroad being constructed alongside it.

Wilmington's growth from the 1860s to the 1960s was tremendous. Its population increased nearly twenty fold from about 700 to over 13,000 during this time. The railroad, streetcar, and later the automobile greatly influenced this rapid growth. In 1875 the town was serviced by four rail lines and four depots. It would be these rail lines and cars of the Eastern Massachusetts Street Railway Co. that would bring hundreds of "city folks" to the camps and cottages of Silver Lake. In 1915 a municipal electric supply was introduced to the town and in 1928 a water department and public water supply was created. The late 1950s would see hundreds of acres of land taken and many homes and farms demolished to make room for a new eight-lane highway. The completion of Interstate 93 in 1960 was a major catalyst in Wilmington's transformation into a "suburban community." The flight of city dwellers from Boston and its environs swelled the town's population. Fields where cows once grazed and crops once grew gave way to cul-de-sacs lined with ranches and split-levels. The industries of the space program and Cold War sprang up everywhere. Wilmington's landscape and rural roots were forever changed.

This photographic history of Wilmington will span from the 1880s to the mid-1960s. Each chapter will focus on a specific aspect of life in Wilmington during that time period. Presented in a chronological order, the photographs will allow the reader to view a flowing history of Wilmington's growth and development. Many lost, forgotten, and never-before-seen images have been brought together to offer the reader a comprehensive look at Wilmington's past.

One
Around the Town

A scene looking north from the Town Common, c. 1898. On the right and from the foreground can be seen Jim Kelley's store, St. Thomas of Villanova Chapel, the Samuel B. Nichols House, and the Congregational church's parsonage. On the left is the Thomas McMahon House, built in the 1840s by Joseph Bond Jr. It was originally located across the street as part of the Bond Cracker Baking Factory.

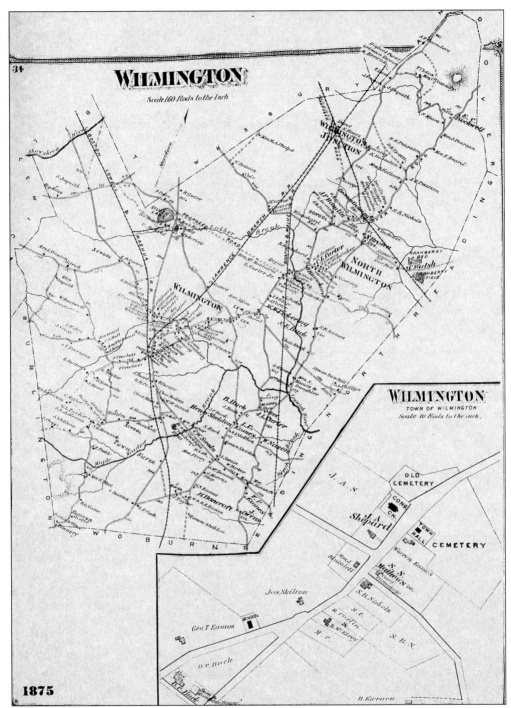

An 1875 map of Wilmington showing in great detail the town's many homes, businesses, roads, rail lines, and schools. The distinctive "mitten" shape of the town is evident here as well. Many of the named houses shown here appear in individual photographs throughout this book.

10

Aldrich Road near Forest Street, c. 1898. Sewall Buck's house on the left was built c. 1812 on property originally settled by Sergeant Abraham Jaquith in 1665. Remnants of the Jaquith House foundation can be seen in the left foreground. Sergeant Jaquith was killed in 1676 during King Philip's War. He was the son of Abraham Jaquith, the progenitor of Jaquiths in America, who settled in Charlestown in 1643.

Shawsheen Avenue or "the road to Billerica," a dirt path not much wider than the horse carts that traveled on it when this 1898 photograph was taken. The Walker House (on the right) was built shortly after the Revolutionary War by Benjamin Walker, father of Timothy Walker and Sears Cook Walker. It was located in the vicinity of the present-day Fred F. Cain Bridge.

(CHAPTER 389)

ACTS OF 1898.

AN ACT RELATIVE TO OFFICIAL SEALS AND CERTIFICATES.

Be it enacted, etc., as follows : —

SECTION 1. The city of Boston shall provide for use by the registrar of births, deaths and marriages of said city an official seal, and said registrar shall attest all certificates from records in his custody with said seal.

SECTION 2. Every town shall provide for the use of its town clerk an official seal, bearing the name of the town and the date of its incorporation, and of such general design as may be approved by the Selectmen thereof.

SECTION 3. Said registrar and every city and town clerk, when furnishing a copy of any record of births, deaths or marriages in his charge, shall furnish the same under the official seal of the city or town, as the case may be.

SECTION 4. This act shall take effect on the first day of January in the year eighteen hundred and ninety-nine. *[Approved April 29, 1898.*

In accordance with the provisions of the above act, the Selectmen of the town of Wilmington, Mass., authorized Mr. Arthur Thomas Bond to prepare a suitable design. Without delay he complied, and March 16th, 1899, submitted for their approval an enlarged copy of seal as shown below. It was approved on March 20th, 1899.

The design represents in the foreground an old tree of historic interest which has stood for several generations near the North Wilmington Station, known as the "Whitefield Elm."

In the background, on the left, is shown the ancient house on the "Esq. Eames place"; on the right are shown modern buildings, with the depot in the distance.

TOWN CLERK'S OFFICE, *April 11th 1899*

A true copy. — *Attest:*

Witness the official seal of the Town of Wilmington, [Middlesex County] Mass.

Town Clerk.

The document that made the seal of the town of Wilmington official. The first time the new town seal, designed by Arthur Thomas Bond, was used was when it was affixed to this document relating to the adoption and use of official seals. In other words, the new seal of the town of Wilmington was used to officiate the document accepting the seal's design.

A winter scene of Main Street dating from c. 1900. Ames Hall (on the right) along with many other area building were destroyed by fire in 1903. Of note are the streetcar tracks which ran down the center of the street. This was done for the safety of patrons entering and exiting stores situated close to the street.

A view of Boutwell Street looking from Carter Lane toward Aldrich Road, c. 1900. The Boutwell House (on the left) was probably built prior to 1710 and was the ancestral home of Civil War-era Massachusetts Governor George Boutwell. The house, which was torn down in 1930, stood opposite the entrance to the Boutwell Street School.

West Street. Prior to the completion of Interstate 93 in 1960 West Street ran uninterrupted from the Reading line to Woburn Street just south of the Ipswich River and was dominated by large expanses of farmland. Characteristic of most areas away from the center of town, the road is winding and narrow and the homes are few and far between.

A horse-drawn cart on muddy, rutted Lowell Street at the turn of the century. The streetcar tracks are barely visible under the overhead electric line on the left.

Looking northeast on Church Street from just south of Clark Street, *c.* 1910. The two homes visible on the left and most of the other houses that still stand on Church Street were built during the period of 1850 to 1910 and represent fine examples of Victorian and Queen Anne-style architecture.

"Buck's Corner" at the intersection of Wildwood and Woburn Streets, named because of the large number of Buck family descendants living in the area. The house in the background to the right of the barn was built in 1671 by Roger Buck and his son Ephraim. It still stands today as the oldest house in town.

A *c.* 1915 photograph of the intersection of Lowell and Woburn Streets, also known as "Perry's Corner." Murray's store (on the left) became John Lucci's original market in the 1950s, and Perry's blacksmith shop can be seen to the right of Murray's. The streetcar tracks go both west along Lowell Street and north to "Buck's Corner."

The area of Burlington Avenue occupied by present-day Dell Drive. This area has changed a great deal from the way it appears in this 1913 photograph, which features members of the Brooks family and one of their cows strolling about the family farm's pastures.

Burlington Avenue, c. 1920, looking toward Chestnut Street from in front of the Fred Roberts Estate (not visible). The cottage on the right was moved to the location shown here from directly across the road when candy maker Fred Roberts built his mansion there in 1912.

Silver Lake. Like Martin's Pond in North Reading and Nutting Lake in Billerica, Wilmington's Silver Lake was a summertime destination for many vacationers from in and around Boston. Conveniently located between a railroad right of way and a streetcar line, the area saw a great influx of people beginning in the late 1890s and continuing through the 1940s.

The Tweed-Manning House as it appeared in the 1930s, when it was owned by Herb Foskett. The 250-year-old house appears to be in remarkable condition. By the 1960s, however, it was standing in the way of progress and was demolished to make room for a new industrial park.

The former Squire Samuel Eames House, made well known through its depiction on the town seal, as it appeared in 1938. Heavily damaged by an arsonist's hand in 1966, it was deemed too costly to repair and was instead demolished.

An unidentified woman adjacent to the brook that passes under the Roman Way (now Adams Street) near the present-day Wilmington High School. The Roman Way was just a dirt path when this 1950 photograph was taken; the area had yet to be developed into the residential neighborhood that stands there today.

The area of town bordered by Main, Cross, Lowell, and Woburn Streets. This area was owned almost entirely by Herb Barrows, who lived in the Perry House (adjacent to Perry's blacksmith shop on Woburn Street). In the late 1950s Herb sold this land to the Avco Research and Advanced Development Division (now Textron), a leading aerospace and defense contractor. The sprawling complex now occupies most of the land seen in this photograph.

The spring thaw of the late 1950s. Jim's Variety, which stood on the corner of Shawsheen Avenue and Hopkins Street, was torn down c. 1970 and the site is now occupied by the 129 Food Mart and Uncle Micky's Pizza.

Main Street just south of Clark Street, c. 1957. Behind the Service Market is Dame's Garage (now the Wilmington House of Pizza). To the rear of the Dodge billboard is the former Shawsheen Avenue Bridge. Although open to motor vehicle traffic when this photograph was taken, it is now a pedestrian bridge.

A busy Main Street scene during the evening commute, c. 1959. The view is from opposite the present-day telephone company building looking south toward Church Street.

A view of Route 62 (Salem Street) where it passes the site of the "Old Nod Saw Mill" on Martin's Brook near the North Reading line. The area in the right foreground adjacent to the dirt path and gate was the location of the sawmill, which was in operation as early as 1695 and appears on town maps of 1794, 1830, 1856, and 1875.

The parts of Wilmington and Tewksbury collectively known as "Silver Lake," c. 1960. Silver Lake, a small, spring-fed kettle pond, has figured prominently in Wilmington's history since the 1850s. Prior to widespread availability and use of electric refrigeration the lake's ice houses enjoyed a booming business. The demand for ice was so great that the Boston and Lowell Railroad Company even built a spur line from their main right of way to the lake to facilitate the transport of this valuable product. Beginning in the early 1900s the lake became a mecca for summer tourists.

Two
Homes

The clapboard house with a stucco front known as the Scales House in 1898. Located on the north side of Salem Street adjacent to the Lawrence branch of the Boston and Lowell Railroad, the house dates back to 1741. It is no longer standing; the date it was torn down is unknown.

The 1889 Queen Anne-style cottage on Middlesex Avenue in North Wilmington. This was the home of Herbert and Emma Buck. The people standing on the porch in this *c.* 1898 photograph are probably Herbert Buck (right) and his son Rodney. Herbert, a descendent of Roger Buck, was one of the owners of Buck Bros. Grocers.

The house labeled O. Eames on an 1875 map of the town. Located on the west side of Woburn Street, just north of the Ipswich River, the house stands across the street from the Caleb Eames House. The family in this *c.* 1890s photograph appears to be dressed up for some type of celebration (note the flag and bunting in the window). Today the house is the Brookside Nursery School.

The Federal-style home of Caleb Eames. The house, located today on Woburn Street just north of the Ipswich River, was built with its front facing south and its side to Woburn Street, which appears in the foreground of this 1898 photograph.

The Roger Buck House, located on "Buck's Corner," as it appeared in 1898. Some accounts of the age of this house put its construction date as early as 1635 but this cannot be corroborated in any way. It is generally accepted that Wilmington's oldest existing house was actually built in 1671 or 1672.

The Perry House on Woburn Street, just south of John Perry's blacksmith shop. This building, built *c.* 1710 by Joseph Winn Jr., was an impeccably maintained, gambrel-roofed house, and was nearly 190 years old when this photograph was taken in 1898. In more recent years it was the home of Herb Barrows and was the property of Avco when it was destroyed by an arson fire in 1965.

The building known in 1898 as the Isaac Damon House. Built *c.* 1760, this structure was located on the southern end of Main Street directly across from present-day Eames Street and just south of the Eames property that made up the Town Poor Farm.

A house described as "the last house on the road to Woburn past Bell Farm." If this is accurate it would put the house on the very southern end of Chestnut Street near the Woburn line. The house appears to be abandoned as is evident from the heavy weathering, boarded up window, and many broken panes of glass.

The Samuel Butters House on Chestnut Street, built in 1712 as a garrison-style house with an overhanging second floor. Shown here in 1898, its original lines had only recently been altered to eliminate the overhang. The house still stands today on the north side of the street between Butters Row and the William Butters II House.

The Dowd House (above) and the Holt-Slack House (below), both originally located on the site of the Fred Roberts Estate on Burlington Avenue. These two houses, along with two others and the land they occupied, were purchased by candy maker Fred Roberts in 1912. Three of the houses were moved and the fourth was demolished in order to make room for his mansion.

The Richard Hopkins House, built *c.* 1734. This building was located on Aldrich Road, about one half mile west of the Sergeant Abraham Jaquith House, when this area of town was still part of Billerica. In 1737 Richard Hopkins was one of seven petitioners to the General Court who succeeded having this section of Billerica set off to Wilmington.

The Ebenezar Pierce/Levi Reynolds House, which stands today at the corner of Middlesex Avenue and Adelaide Street. This building was built in 1716 and originally stood at the corner of Butters Row and Main Street. It was moved to its present location in the early 1800s and its roof line was changed to a gambrel style shortly after this 1898 photograph was taken.

The Squire William Blanchard Jr. House, nestled behind the oaks, elms, and maples at the corner of Glen Road and Middlesex Avenue. In the early 1800s Squire Blanchard was one of the town's wealthiest residents as he was paid the generous salary of $2,000 for his position as state inspector of hops.

A house probably built c. 1725 by Benjamin Harnden. This was the home of Town Clerk Samuel Eames in the early 1800s. It was located on the west side of Middlesex Avenue just south of the North Wilmington train depot. Reading Co-operative Bank now occupies the site.

The Stimpson House on Salem Street, often described as "the last house on Flint Street by Tewksbury." For reasons unknown to the author, Salem Street was known as Flint Street in the late 1800s. This *c.* 1780 house still stands, although its roof line has been altered and the house was lengthened by adding a two-story extension to the left of the front door.

The Lieutenant Jonathan Jones House on Andover Street near Foster's Pond, probably built before 1720. Of note are the ground-floor windows on the right which are smaller than the windows on the left. Lieutenant Jones and his son, Ensign Jonathan Jones, served with His Majesty's naval forces on Lake George in New York during the French and Indian War.

The Newton George House on Ballardvale Street, located in the vicinity of the present-day Interstate 93/Route 125 interchange. This building stood adjacent to, and just south of, the bridge over the tracks of the now defunct Salem and Lowell Railroad. It was the last house on Ballardvale Street before reaching the Tweed-Manning House.

The Tweed-Manning House. Although no longer standing, this was probably the third oldest house in town when this photograph was taken in 1898. Built c. 1685 on Ballardvale Street, its approximate location was on the right side of the road about one half mile north of Route 125.

The Pearson Tavern on the corner of Salem and Ballardvale Street. This was the home of Aaron Pearson Jr., the son of Major Aaron Pearson (who commanded troops from Massachusetts during the War of 1812). It was the second house on "the road to Salem" that is known to have operated as a tavern, the other being the Harnden Tavern located one half mile east on the corner of Woburn Street.

The Fourth of July House (or the 1776 House) on Andover Street, so named because its timber frame is said to have been raised by Ebenezar Jones on July 4, 1776. Originally built as a smaller, gambrel-roofed cottage, it faces southeast toward the Brown's Crossing Pumping Station.

The Boutwell House on Boutwell Street. This was originally the home of Giles Roberds or Roberts and was probably built by him *c.* 1700–10. This *c.* 1900 view is from Boutwell Street looking at the north corner of the house. The house was small even for its day, the gambrel-roofed section being only slightly larger than a modern-day tool shed.

The Carter House on Lowell Street. Built in the 1860s, the building still stands today across from Lucci's Shopping Center. This *c.* 1908 photograph shows a young Olive Mae Carter (left) and her brother Kenneth sitting on the front steps. Olive would later marry Wilbur Sheldon, son of Asa G. Sheldon (1862–1939). She was widowed in 1927 when Wilbur, a Wilmington fireman, was killed while fighting a fire at Silver Lake.

The William E. Gowing House on Andover Street in North Wilmington, just east of Brown's Crossing.

The Eldad Carter House. Located on the corner of Shawsheen Avenue and Bridge Lane for over two hundred years, this building was built around the time of the Revolutionary War. Although gone from this location it was thankfully not demolished; instead, it was systematically dismantled and trucked out of town by its new owner in the early 1990s for reassembly elsewhere.

The Hudson/Roman House on Church Street, c. 1930, elaborately decorated for some patriotic celebration. It is shown here in a seldom seen view from the side yard. This grand, Queen Anne-style house was built in 1897 and featured a large veranda, conical turret, widows walk,

and meticulously landscaped grounds. This house is now property of the town, serving as the school department's administration building.

The Boutwell House, in a sad state of disrepair and quite possibly abandoned. It was torn down shortly after this c. 1930 photograph was taken.

The Fred Roberts Estate on Burlington Avenue. Known as "The Boulders" when it was built, it featured this large house, a barn, silo, windmill, and beautiful flower gardens. This photograph shows the house as it looked when it was built, which is also how it appears today, as its outer appearance has remained virtually unchanged for over eighty years.

Three
Businesses

The Bond Cracker Baking Factory, located on Middlesex Avenue near the present-day Baptist church. The factory was started by Captain Joseph Bond of Woburn when he moved to Wilmington in 1802, and it produced the famous Bond Crackers at this location until a devastating fire destroyed the bake houses in 1864. The Bond family chose to not to rebuild the factory and moved their business to Boston shortly after the fire.

The Perry, Cutler, and Co. Tannery. This business, which opened in 1856, produced leather used to make shoes for the Union Army during the Civil War. The young boy pictured on the left with his mother in this 1885 photograph is future owner Caleb Harriman, who took over the business in 1900. The tannery ceased operations in 1950 and its buildings were razed in 1961.

A drawing of Harriman's Tannery showing in great detail how the business looked at the turn of the century. Middlesex Avenue is in the foreground, the settling ponds are to the right, and the Boston and Maine Railroad can be seen in the background.

A photograph of two of the buildings of the Bond Cracker Baking Factory, which appears in the painting on p.39. As evident from the streetcar tracks in the foreground, these two buildings survived the fire of 1864 and stood until at least the late 1890s. No longer standing, the time and reason for their demise is unknown.

Captain Joseph Bond (1761–1840). Captain Bond was born in Gloucester and served in the Revolutionary War as a private from 1777 to 1779. He was a baker's apprentice in Boston in 1789 and began his own business shortly after moving to Wilmington. His rank title comes from the fact that he commanded the East Militia Company of Woburn as a captain from 1799 to 1801.

41

The 1898 remains of the Samuel Jaques Grist Mill, which he built in 1769 on Settle Meadow Brook just west of the Reverend Isaac Morrill House. Jaques probably did not build his mill new but more than likely made larger the existing Daniel Snow Mill, which was built *c.* 1705.

The Town Poor Farm, located on Main Street south of the Boston and Lowell Railroad. The poor farm was originally owned by the Eames family. During the late 1800s it was used to house indigent and invalid residents of Wilmington, who were allowed to grow and sell produce as a means of earning money and maintaining the property.

John W. Perry's blacksmith shop at the corner of Woburn and Lowell Streets, c. 1898. The shop was originally built in Boston by Asa G. Sheldon (1788–1870) so that he would have a steady supply of shoes for his teams of oxen he was using to cut down Pemberton Hill and fill in the Back Bay. When he had finished the job he moved the shop to Wilmington.

Burly John W. Perry, son of John S. Perry, at work in his blacksmith shop at the turn of the century.

Thompson's Saw Mill, located just east of Silver Lake in the area of land bounded by Main Street and Glen Road. The mill derived its power from a small pond that was fed by both Lubber's Brook and run off from Silver Lake. Like most of the mills in town it dates from the early 1700s and quite possibly before. The early settlers of the town were keen to take advantage

of the water power available to them and built mills on the Shawsheen River, the Ipswich River, Maple Meadow Brook, Settle Meadow Brook, Lubber's Brook, and Martin's Brook. Abandoned, falling apart, and surrounded by overgrown vegetation, the mill had seen better days by the time this c. 1890s photograph was taken.

The Isaac Carter House on the corner of Clark Street and Middlesex Avenue. This building was built c. 1720 but its original lines are obscured by later additions and alterations. During the later part of the nineteenth century Willie Eames ran a store from this location, selling among other things "tonics and medicines." More than likely Willie was using his store to peddle some homemade liquor.

The Nichols Funeral Home on the corner of Middlesex Avenue and Wildwood Street, c. 1900. This house dates from the 1760s and stands adjacent to the former site of the Bond Cracker Baking Factory.

Noah Clapp's sawmill at the turn of this century. All that remained when this photograph was taken was the great stone dam and a few rotting timbers. Located on the end of Mill Road at the base of Wood Hill, it was powered by the waters of Mill Brook. The beams for the Congregational church built in 1865 are said to have come from this mill.

The 1880s home of sawmill owner Noah Clapp. This diminutive Cape Cod-style house was built about the time of the Revolutionary War by Ebenezar Foster. It still stands today on Burlington Avenue just west of Dell Drive.

The Bedell Bros. Insurance Building (now Caddell and Byers Insurance) on Main Street, c. 1903, when it was the Wilmington Post Office. This building, which was used as a post office until new quarters were built on the corner of Main and Church Streets in the mid-1950s, was originally built by France B. Hiller for her husband, Henry Hiller II, to use as a real estate office.

Masonic Temple, Wilmington, Mass.

The one-time laboratory of Henry and France B. Hiller. This structure had become the Masonic Temple by the time this 1907 photograph was taken. It was from this building that the Drs. Hiller amassed much of their fortune from a prosperous pharmaceutical business.

The north side of the Boston and Maine Railroad tracks in North Wilmington, c. 1918. Buck Bros. Grocers (now Elia's Country Store) is adjacent to the tracks while the North Wilmington Post Office can be seen in the background. In addition to being a general store, Buck Bros. also served as Wilmington's central exchange for the New England Telephone and Telegraph Co. (note the Bell sign over the door).

Rocco's Restaurant, opened by Rocco DePasquale Sr. on July 4, 1940. It is located on Main Street just south of Silver Lake and has been continuously operated by the DePasquale family for over fifty-seven years.

Rocco DePasquale Sr. (center) and his family about the time he opened his restaurant.

Two views of Carter's Garage at the intersection of Lowell and Main Streets. These images show the business as it appeared *c.* 1945 (above) and in 1954 (below), after Hurricane Carol roared up the East Coast and smashed into Massachusetts. Notice in the bottom photograph that the car adjacent to the gas pumps has been completely crushed by the fallen facade. The building was repaired and is the present-day home of A & S Towing.

The new location of John Lucci's store. When Lucci vacated his first store (the former Murray's store, pictured on p. 16) in the mid-1950s he moved next door to this new block and the old store was demolished. The cupola on Herb Barrow's barn on Woburn Street can be seen behind the Beautirama salon on the right.

A 1958 aerial view looking south over the recently opened Avco Research and Advanced Development Division complex, located on property formerly owned by Herb Barrows. Lowell Street is in the foreground, Woburn Street is shown in the upper left, and Eames Street is in the extreme background.

Four
Churches

The Reverend Isaac Morrill House, located on Middlesex Avenue just north of the Settle Meadow Brook. This building was built by Daniel Snow in 1703. Reverend Morrill was Wilmington's second—and ultimately its most popular—minister. He took over the church from the Reverend James Varney in 1741 and served until his death in 1793. This photograph shows the house as it appeared in 1898.

The United Church of Christ (the First Congregational Church). This is Wilmington's oldest religious congregation, having been organized in 1733. The structure shown in this *c.* 1900 photograph was built in 1865 and is the third Congregational church building.

The parsonage of the Congregational church on the corner of Middlesex Avenue and Wildwood Street. This house once belonged to the Bond family, whose bakery was located on the opposite corner of Wildwood Street, adjacent to the Samuel B. Nichols House. Note the streetcar tracks making the bend toward "Buck's Corner."

The 1841 Free Will Baptist Society building. In 1824 the church and town government split up and became two separate entities. Not long after that, Wilmington's second religious organization, the Free Will Baptist Society, formed. Their church was built in 1841 and was used until the congregation dissolved around the time of the Civil War. The building later served as a high school, town hall, and, most recently, as the Wilmington Council for the Arts Building.

A building that was formerly part of the Bond Cracker Baking Factory on Middlesex Avenue. This structure was moved across the street to its present location by Albert Bond, son of Joseph Bond Jr. It was from the upstairs front room of this house that Wilmington's first Catholic Mass was celebrated in 1884.

The section of the Wildwood Cemetery that faces Middlesex Avenue. This section began to be used c. 1795–1800, after the original burying ground beside the town's meetinghouse became overcrowded. The box-like brick structure in the upper right is a memorial to the Reverend Isaac Morrill.

The Methodist Episcopal Church building, c. 1950. The Methodist Episcopal Church traces its history in Wilmington back to 1880, when people of this religious faith began meeting in private homes for worship. In 1883 the church was incorporated and the following year the building shown here was erected. It served as the congregation's place of worship until 1957, when the current church was built.

The Congregation Ahavash Achim Daaron, established by Harry Modelevsky, Jacob Cheifitz, Joshua Cohen, Harry Solow, Morris Modelevsky, Joseph Minsky, Hyman Minsky, and Jacob Winer in the months preceding Rosh Hashanah, 1917. The Salem Street temple, shown here c. 1960, became Temple Shalom in the late 1960s and closed in 1978 due to a decline in Wilmington's Jewish population. It is now a private dwelling.

St. Mary's Chapel, located on Vernon Street in Tewksbury. Although Masses had been held both out of doors and in the hall at Thompson's Grove, it wasn't until St. Mary's Chapel was built that the large Irish-Catholic population of Silver Lake had an actual church (although not a parish) they could call their own.

St. Dorothy's Church. The parish of St. Dorothy was established in 1954 to serve the people of West Wilmington, Silver Lake, and South Tewksbury. The church shown here was built in 1959 and stands on the corner of Main and Harnden Streets.

The Kingdom Hall of Jehovah's Witnesses on the corner of Bridge Lane and Brand Avenue. This house of worship, although still standing and in use, was extensively modified and enlarged in the early 1990s and now bears little resemblance to the way it appears in this c. 1960 photograph.

The second Methodist church, built in 1957 adjacent to the site of the first church.

The St. Thomas of Villanova Church. This chapel was built in 1888 and served as an Augustinian mission church until the Archbishop of Boston, William Cardinal O'Connell, set aside Wilmington as a separate parish in 1919. Shown here in 1960, the building was demolished in 1968 to make room for the new Wilmington Memorial Library.

The new St. Thomas of Villanova Church. The new structure was built in 1960 on Middlesex Avenue on the grounds of the former Thomas Davis Bond Estate. Its white facade, glassed belfry, and narrow spire gives it an appearance similar to that of the First Congregational Church.

Five
Schools

East School children pose outside *c.* 1888 for a group photograph with their teacher, Miss Abbie Sheldon. After teaching for only a short time, Miss Sheldon resigned and married Charles Sargent in October of 1891. She is the mother of long-time Water Department Superintendent Edmund "Eddie" Sargent.

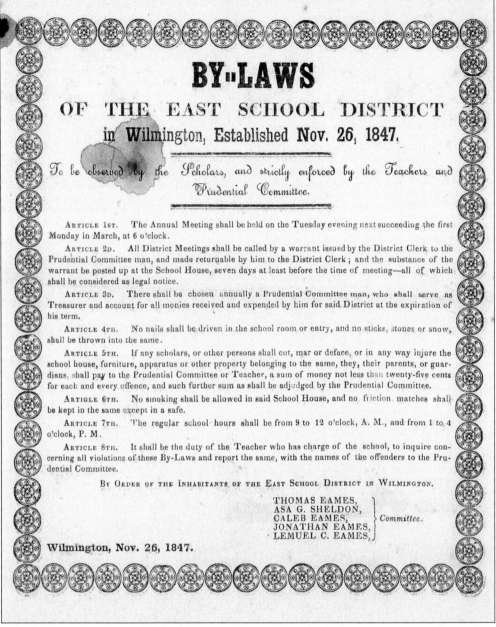

BY-LAWS

OF THE EAST SCHOOL DISTRICT
in Wilmington, Established Nov. 26, 1847.

To be observed by the Scholars, and strictly enforced by the Teachers and Prudential Committee.

ARTICLE 1ST. The Annual Meeting shall be held on the Tuesday evening next succeeding the first Monday in March, at 6 o'clock.

ARTICLE 2D. All District Meetings shall be called by a warrant issued by the District Clerk to the Prudential Committee man, and made returnable by him to the District Clerk; and the substance of the warrant be posted up at the School House, seven days at least before the time of meeting—all of which shall be considered as legal notice.

ARTICLE 3D. There shall be chosen annually a Prudential Committee man, who shall serve as Treasurer and account for all monies received and expended by him for said District at the expiration of his term.

ARTICLE 4TH. No nails shall be driven in the school room or entry, and no sticks, stones or snow, shall be thrown into the same.

ARTICLE 5TH. If any scholars, or other persons shall cut, mar or deface, or in any way injure the school house, furniture, apparatus or other property belonging to the same, they, their parents, or guardians, shall pay to the Prudential Committee or Teacher, a sum of money not less than twenty-five cents for each and every offence, and such further sum as shall be adjudged by the Prudential Committee.

ARTICLE 6TH. No smoking shall be allowed in said School House, and no friction matches shall be kept in the same except in a safe.

ARTICLE 7TH. The regular school hours shall be from 9 to 12 o'clock, A. M., and from 1 to 4 o'clock, P. M.

ARTICLE 8TH. It shall be the duty of the Teacher who has charge of the school, to inquire concerning all violations of these By-Laws and report the same, with the names of the offenders to the Prudential Committee.

BY ORDER OF THE INHABITANTS OF THE EAST SCHOOL DISTRICT IN WILMINGTON.

THOMAS EAMES,
ASA G. SHELDON,
CALEB EAMES, } *Committee.*
JONATHAN EAMES,
LEMUEL C. EAMES,

Wilmington, Nov. 26, 1847.

The by-laws for the East School District of Wilmington as set forth in 1847. Up until state laws abolished school districts in 1869 Wilmington was divided into five such sections. The North, South, East, West, and Central Districts each had their own governing body which established the rules and regulations for their particular school.

A *c.* 1895 photograph showing the children of the East School, this time with teacher Miss Henrietta Ames Swain. Born in Wilmington in 1873, Etta Swain was trained at the Salem Normal School after graduation from Wilmington High School. She assumed her teaching duties at the East School in 1893.

Miss Etta Swain with her students inside the East School in 1897. Etta, along with her sister Carrie, would both teach in various Wilmington schools for a combined total of almost eighty years. They were daughters of Charles W. Swain, founder of the Wilmington Public Library.

The Old Centre School, c. 1900. Built for the Central School District in 1839, the Old Centre School is the oldest existing school building in town. The one-room school became the Wilmington Public Library in 1899 and served as such until the current library opened in 1969.

The East School as it appeared in 1900. Located on the corner of Federal and Woburn Streets, it is now a private dwelling. This is a mirror image of the school. The dirt road shown here on the right side of the school is Federal Street, which actually runs along the left side of the school.

The North School, built in 1868 in the "Land of Nod." The school stood at the corner of Salem and Ballardvale Streets in North Wilmington and was demolished in the early 1960s to make room for the North Intermediate School, a modern, multi-room junior high school.

Walker School children pose outside in 1901 with their teacher, Miss Sylvia Prescott. Marion Carter Cole, later Marion Connor (front row, second from left), was for many years Wilmington's oldest resident. She passed away during the production of this book just a few days shy of her 106th birthday.

Two c. 1903 Center School class photographs. The top photograph shows the children against the fence with the McMahon House (formerly the Albert Bond House) chimneys barely visible above the trees on the left. The bottom photograph shows the children along the side of the Wilmington Public Library. Philip Buzzell, the son of school physician Dr. Daniel Buzzell, appears in both photographs (in the top photograph he is sitting on ground, third from left; in the bottom image, he is in the back row, second from right).

The Whitefield School, built in 1906 and shown here *c.* 1910. This was Wilmington's third multi-room school after the Center School (1888) and the Walker School (1896). It is located on Middlesex Avenue on the property of the former estate of Squire Samuel Eames and now serves as quarters for the Wilmington Public Buildings Department.

Walker School children from the 1912–13 school year on the front steps of the school. Their teacher (back row, third from left) is former East School teacher Etta Swain.

The Swain School. When the town's growing student population necessitated the building of a new high school, a two-story, multi-room brick building was constructed on the corner of School Street and Middlesex Avenue. Shown here under construction in 1914, it would later be named for sisters Carrie and Etta Swain.

The Center School (the former high school). Wilmington's first multi-room school building was constructed in 1888 adjacent to the Old Centre School and is shown here as it appeared in 1916. The building was demolished in the early 1980s, after it was decided that it was no longer being suitable for use as a school.

The Wilmington High School Class of 1916.

Elementary school-age children outside Wilmington High School in the early 1920s. These children are possibly from the Center School, which was located next to the high school and was being used as an elementary school during this time.

Students and teachers on the steps of Wilmington High School on Middlesex Avenue, *c.* 1920. By the late 1940s this building had become completely overcrowded and another "new" high school would be needed.

The Wilmington High School Class of 1924.

The West School on Shawsheen Avenue. This school was built sometime after 1875 to replace the original West School District's building, which stood across the street on the corner of Aldrich Road. Shown here in the late 1940s the West School is now on the National Register of Historic Places and is currently undergoing extensive interior and exterior renovations.

The new Wilmington High School on Church Street, c. 1955. To the left of the school is the Roman House with its carriage house in the rear. The Class of 1951 was the first class to

graduate from this building. It has been renovated several times since opening, and it still serves today as the town's only high school.

A look inside the Wilmington Public Library when it was housed in the Old Centre School. In the background can be seen photographs of Anna Tolman Sheldon, who served as librarian from 1900 to 1938, and Dr. Daniel Buzzell, the longtime school physician.

The Wildwood Street School shortly after its opening in 1955. The Wildwood was the first of several new schools built in the 1950s and '60s to educate the children of the post-World War II "baby boom." Others that were built during this time period were the Glen Road School, the Boutwell School, the Woburn Street School, the North Intermediate School, the West Intermediate School, and the Shawsheen School.

Six
The Police Department

Chief Walter Hill (far left) and officers of the Wilmington Police Department in front of the Wilmington Highway Department's garage on Adelaide Street in 1929. In addition to providing garage space for the town's police car this building also housed the department's lock-up facilities. The steel cage cell can be seen inside the open bay door.

Officer Francis S. "Nifty" Hoban and Officer Benjamin Solow in front of their patrol car on Church Street. In 1939 town-wide motorized patrols were introduced. The building above the car with the sign that reads "Cement and Lumber" would be converted into the police station in the early 1940s.

Officer Hoban and Chairman of the Board of Selectmen Charles Black. Hoban is being congratulated by Black for his courageous efforts in capturing a robber who held up the Mechanics Savings Bank on Main Street in 1939. This ceremony took place at the town hall and was attended by the entire police force along with the board of selectmen, Mechanics Savings Bank officials, and Middlesex County District Attorney Robert Bradford.

Chief Harry Ainsworth and regular officers outside their new headquarters on Church Street, c. 1940. The department would occupy this building until 1953.

The special (auxiliary) officers outside the Church Street station, c. 1940. In addition to his regular officers, Chief Ainsworth could rely on the "specials" if extra manpower was ever needed.

Chief Ainsworth at the wheel of the town's new Cadillac ambulance. This vehicle was acquired in 1941 to replace a second-hand Lincoln that had been in service since 1934. The Shell employee is obviously pleased with the new vehicle.

Chief Harry Ainsworth, who headed the Wilmington Police Department from 1932 until 1947. Chief Ainsworth is shown here about the time of his departure to become probation officer at Woburn District Court.

Chief Hoban. After Chief Ainsworth's resignation in 1947 Deputy Chief Hoban temporarily assumed command of the department. He is shown here leading a late 1940s Memorial Day parade down Church Street.

Officer Charlie Ellsworth with the department's safety car. This vehicle was donated by Fred F. Cain's Chrysler dealership. The building in the background is the Wilmington Public Library on Middlesex Avenue.

School Traffic Supervisor Maryann Langone at the north corner of Church and Main Streets, c. 1955. Whistle in hand, she is ready to face the town's ever increasing traffic and safety concerns.

A photograph taken for the 1956 Annual Town Report. Chief Paul Lynch (center, civilian clothes) poses here along with police officers and traffic supervisors on the stage of an unidentified school.

The new and current police station under construction in 1960. In 1953 a combined police and fire station was built on Church Street adjacent to the town's original fire station. However, failure to plan for the town's growth made this facility obsolete in just seven short years. The new and current police station, shown here under construction in 1960, was built on Adelaide Street on the site of the former town garage.

School Traffic Supervisor Sergeant Maryann Langone (center) and her charges on the front steps of the police station in 1962. These woman were trained by the Registry of Motor Vehicles' Division of Safety Education in current traffic laws and school safety techniques.

A much larger department outside their new quarters on Adelaide Street, *c.* 1962 This modern, state-of-the-art building was dedicated in 1961 and it featured abundant office space, modern bathroom and shower facilities, a kitchen, and an indoor pistol range. It currently serves as the town's police station but is slated to be replaced by another combined police and fire station in 1999.

Officer John "Leo" Markey (left) and Officer James "Jay" Palmer with their cruisers in front of the police station in 1963. Both officers, although deceased, served on the department for a combined total of more than sixty years.

Seven
The Fire Department

The Wilmington Fire Department's Engine Co. One and Hose One outside their Church Street quarters. Following a devastating 1903 fire that destroyed many buildings in the center of town, it was decided that a well-equipped and manned fire department was needed. Of interest is the fact that uniforms had not been obtained yet, which suggests this photograph was taken probably no later than 1904.

A 1906 photograph of the fire department's North Wilmington contingent. Engine Co. Two and Hose Two formed the fire department's North Wilmington contingent in the early 1900s. They were housed on the grounds of Harriman's Tannery which was a task easily accomplished due to the fact that Caleb Harriman was chief of the department. By the time this photo was taken the men sported fancy uniforms featuring white trousers and shirts emblazoned with the number "2."

Engine Co. One and Hose One on the grounds of the Masonic Temple on Church Street, *c.* 1915. Four years later the horses would be gone as the department obtained its first piece of motorized equipment.

Fireman Wilbur Sheldon. Tragically, Fireman Sheldon was killed along with Fireman Russell Pratt while fighting a house fire near Silver Lake in 1927. Both hosemen died when a stream of water was inadvertently directed at the house's red hot chimney, causing the bricks to collapse on top of them.

Members of the Wilmington Fire Department with their apparatus outside the Church Street headquarters in 1940.

Another devastating fire in downtown Wilmington. The above and below photographs show Wilmington firefighters battling the blaze that engulfed McLaughlin's Drug Store in 1947. This wooden structure was almost completely destroyed and would later be replaced by a brick structure of similar size.

The new Wilmington Police and Fire Station on Church Street under construction, *c.* 1952 The original fire station with its many "improvements and additions" can be seen in the immediate background.

The Church Street Station with all the apparatus parked outside their respective bays in 1955. It was about this time that the fire department took over the town's ambulance duties from the police department. This building still serves as the town's only fire station.

Chief Arthur Boudreau (front row, third from left) and fire department personnel inside their new Church Street quarters. *c.* 1956.

Down with the old. The structure that originally housed the Wilmington Fire Department's Engine Co. One and Hose One is shown here being dismantled in the late 1950s. When first constructed the building was so small there was only room for the two pieces of horse-drawn equipment. There was neither sleeping quarters for the men nor stables for the horses.

Eight
Public Works

Land being cleared around the site of the planned Brown's Crossing Pumping Station on Andover Street in North Wilmington. In 1928 the newly formed Wilmington Water Department began the awesome task of creating a public water supply and bringing that water to the residents of the town.

Early-model gas and diesel shovels digging trenches for the new water mains during the summer of 1928. In the above photograph new pipes lie adjacent to the trench being dug on Main Street in front of the Dr. Daniel Buzzell House (now Cavanaugh's Funeral Home). In the photograph below, another shovel struggles with huge boulders on Grant Street. In less than a year over 21 miles of cast-iron water mains were laid and over one hundred customer connections were made all for $2,000 less than the $350,000 appropriated for the project.

The Shawsheen Avenue water main. Unlike today, vehicular traffic on Wilmington's roads in 1928 was not a major concern and work on the Shawsheen Avenue water main is shown here progressing smoothly. The house in the background still stands today and is located on the corner of Shawsheen Avenue and Carter Lane.

One of the Bessemer diesel engines that would power the pumps at the Brown's Crossing station. The engines for the new pumping station were delivered on June 29, 1928.

Three-foot-wide steel plates used to form the Kelley Hill standpipe reservoir on Nassau Avenue. These plates were formed into rings about 30 feet in diameter and were then placed on top of one another to form the standpipe reservoir. Built by the Chicago Bridge and Iron Works Co., the 125-foot-tall, 660,000-gallon tank is still in use after nearly seventy years.

The newly completed Brown's Crossing Pumping Station on Andover Street. Water department employees pose along with the pipe truck and service wagon, the emergency service truck, and the superintendent's car. From left to right are Mr. McQuaide, Art Williams, Elmer Eaton, Superintendent Donald Foster, and Joseph McMahon. A man identified as Mr. Spaulding also appears here.

A WPA project of the mid-1930s. This stone building under construction in the Wildwood Cemetery is now the department of public works' cemetery division office.

A clamshell bucket dredging around the old Nod Dam before reconstruction begins. In the late 1950s the Nod Dam on Martin's Brook in North Wilmington was rebuilt. This dam allows the waters of Martin's Brook to be held back so they may flood the well field around Brown's Crossing. The original dam dates from the late 1690s when the Nod Saw Mill stood here.

Superintendent of Streets James White at the wheel of his truck in front of the town garage on Adelaide Street, c. 1957. Mr. White started working for the highway department in the early 1930s and retired as the department head in 1968. One of his first jobs was paving Burlington Avenue with sheets of oil-soaked denim. Because of this, the road was referred to as "Cotton Street" for many years.

Edmund "Eddie" Sargent, superintendent of the water department, looking over a plan book at the town hall on Middlesex Avenue in 1959.

Nine
Transportation

An open-air trolley stopped at "Perry's Corner," *c.* 1900. Pictured, from left to right, are Katy Murray, Bessie McMahon, Bill "Steamboat" Parker, Rose McMahon, and Alice McMahon. Bill got his nickname because of his high-pitched voice, which sounded like a steam whistle.

Another trolley of the Winchester and Woburn Line at an unknown location in Wilmington. Standing alongside is Charles Sargent (the father of Eddie Sargent), and sitting next to the motorman is Rudolph Porter.

The stone pier that supported the Middlesex Canal aqueduct over the Shawsheen River as seen from Shawsheen Avenue in 1898. Work on the canal began with surveying the land between the Merrimack River and Charlestown in the early 1790s and continued with actual digging and carting away of fill until the waterway opened in 1803.

A view from the Shawsheen River aqueduct crossing looking east along the canal bed. Although out of use for more than sixty years by the time this photograph was taken in 1898, the canal still appears to be navigable.

The stone works of the Shawsheen River aqueduct crossing, c. 1900. The view is looking upstream toward the Shawsheen Avenue Bridge.

The Maple Meadow Brook aqueduct. Although not as tall and elaborate as the Shawsheen River aqueduct, the Maple Meadow Brook aqueduct served the purpose of letting the path of the canal cross over this natural body of water.

The North Wilmington Train Depot, c. 1900. Jonathan Carter's store (in the background) and the train depot (on the left) were destroyed by fire in the early 1900s. It seems that the wood shake roofs of these building were prone to burning, especially when the boilers of passing locomotives constantly showered them with glowing embers and hot ashes.

The busy North Wilmington Train Depot on Middlesex Avenue, c. 1912. On the left, barely visible, is Buck Bros. Grocers (now Elia's Country Store) which was built after the original store on this site burned down in 1904. Only a few years after this photograph was taken many horse-drawn carriages around town began to be replaced by automobiles.

The Silver Lake depot at the end of Wild Avenue. Silver Lake was a popular site to visit for many summer vacationers from in and around Boston. The depot building, shown here c. 1918, was located on the Boston and Lowell (later Boston and Maine) mainline between Lubber's Brook and Lake Street.

A rare view of the Brown's Crossing depot on the now defunct Salem and Lowell Railroad, c. 1927. This was one of five train depots that once serviced Wilmington. The other stops were Wilmington Center, Silver Lake, North Wilmington, and Wilmington Junction.

Wilmington Water Department employee Art Williams operating a hand car on the Salem and Lowell Railroad, c. 1928. When the tracks were clear and the weather was nice Art was able take the hand car from the pumping station at Brown's Crossing a short distance to his house on Andover Street.

Ed Sargent's 1918 Ford Coupe, which he bought secondhand from Roger Buck. The taillight and the lights below the windshield were actually kerosene lamps that were lit by hand when it got dark.

The Wilmington Center depot and freight house as seen from the Burlington Avenue Bridge in the late 1940s. Although still a busy commuter rail stop, the freight house is gone and the depot is now Big Joe's Pizza and Subs. The tracks shown here are part of the oldest existing railroad right of way in the United States, being in continuous use since 1835.

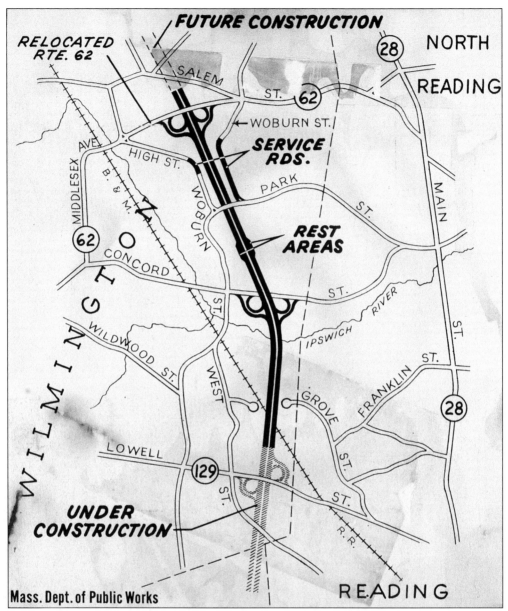

A Massachusetts Department of Public Works plan from the late 1950s showing current and future construction of Interstate 93. The highway cut a swath along the east side of town, causing dozens of homes to be moved or demolished. In addition, several roads were either turned into dead ends or their routes relocated.

Two huge shovels on the future path of Interstate 93, waiting to carve away more of Wilmington's landscape.

An aerial view of Interstate 93's path of construction or destruction, depending on one's point of view. This view is of the Route 62 interchange looking north. It appears the work has reached Salem Street, which would soon be cut through and dead ended on both sides of the highway. The same would hold true for Andover Street a few hundred yards to the north.

The recently completed Interstate 93/Route 129 interchange looking east along Route 129 from the Reading line. The bare patch of land surrounded by the circular on/off ramp in the foreground and the cul-de-sac just above it is the former path of Lowell Street.

The Billerica-Wilmington Airport, located where Hopkins Street crosses into Billerica and becomes Alexander Road. These planes are lined up with their tails toward that road. Closed since the late 1950s, the author remembers playing in the abandoned Quonset Hut-type hangars as a child. The area is now a small industrial park, the only remnant of the airport being the concrete slab foundation of one of the hangars.

Ten
Agriculture

The Silas Brown Farm, *c.* 1900, as viewed looking east toward North Reading. Built by Joshua Harnden in 1770, the main house operated as a tavern from 1794 until 1807. In 1818 the property came into the ownership of Silas Brown and remained in his family for the next 125 years. It was from Silas Brown that Brown's Crossing just north of the farm gets its name.

THE FARMERS' AND MECHANICS' CLUB,

Of WILMINGTON, MIDDLESEX Co., MASS.,

Will hold their FIFTH ANNUAL FAIR & CATTLE SHOW

At WILMINGTON, on the 19th day of September, 1879.

Full particulars to be made known in a Mammoth Poster, which will be issued in the latter part of August, 1879.

The following Premiums are offered :

Fruit and Vegetables.

For the best collection of Apples..........$1.50
" second best " 1.00
For the best plate of Hubbardston Apples.. 50
" " " Sudbury sweet " .. 50
" " " Porter " .. 50
" " " Baldwin " .. 50
" best collection of Pears 1 50
" second best " 1.00
" best plate of " 50
" best collection of Cranberries 1.00
" second best " 50
" best collection of Peaches 1.00
" second best " 50
" best collection of Grapes 1.50
" second best " 1.00
" best bushel of Potatoes.............1.50
" second best " 1.00
" best bushel of Carrots 1.00
" " Parsnips 1 00
" " Beets.................1 00
" " Tomatoes............1 00
" " Egg Plants..........1 00
" " Rutabagas..........1 00
" " Mangolds...........1 00
" " Globe Turnips......1 00
" " Purple Top Turnip..1.00
" " Onions..............1 00
" specimens of Hops 1 00
" Beans 1 00
" half dozen Water Melons 1 00
" half dozen Cantaloupes....... ....1 00
" half dozen Turban Squashes......1 00
" half dozen Hubbard Squashes......1 00
" half dozen Marrow Squashes......1 00
" half dozen Butman's Squashes.....1 00
" half dozen Pumpkins.................1 00
" half dozen Cabbages 1 00
" half dozen Cauliflowers............1 00
" best collection of Vegetables......4 00
" second best " 3 00
" third best " 2 00
For the best collection of Vegetables raised by a boy under 14 years of age.....2 00

Seed Grain.

For the best specimen of Sweet Corn 1 00
" " " Field Corn 1 00
" " " Pop Corn 1 00
" " " Spring Rye 1 00
" " " Winter Rye.......1 00

Bread.

For best specimen of home made Bread $1 50
" second best ...."........."....1 00
" best Rye and Indian Bread.........1 00
" second best " 50

Butter.

For the best specimen of Butter, not less than 6 pounds.................$2 00
" second best........................1 00

Flowers.

For the best exhibition of Flowers........$1 50
" second best.......................1 00
" best exhibition of Wild Flowers ..1 00
" best Bouquet of Flowers........1 00

Prepared Fruits, Pickles & Honey.

For the best collection...................$1 50
" second best 1.00

Working Oxen.

For the best Pair........................$2.00

Milch Cows.

For the best Milch Cow...................$3.00
" second best " 2.00

Bulls, Heifers and Calves.

For the best Bull........................$2.00
" second best Bull.....................1.00
" best Bull Calf.......................1.00
" best Heifer under 3 years.........2.50
" second best " 2.00
" best Heifer under 2 years.........2.00
" second best " 1.50
" best Heifer Calf under 1 year......1.50
" second best " " 1.00

Herds of Cattle.

For the best herd of Cattle of not less than six........................$5.00
" second best " 3.00

Herds of Milch Cows.

For the best herd of Milch Cows of not less than three...................$3.00

Horses.

For the best pair of Farm Horses..........$4.00
" second best " 2.00
" best Farm Horse....................2.00
" second best " 1.50
" best Family and Driving Horse....2.00
" second best " 1.50
" best Colt 3 or 4 years old.........2.00
" best " 2 years and under.......2.00
" best Breeding Mare, with foal by her side.........................3.00

Swine.

For the best Boar.........................$2.00
" best Breeding Sow...................2.00
" best Porker.....................2.00
" best Pig from 3 to 8 months old....2.00

Sheep.

For the best flock of Sheep of not less than six..............................2.00

Poultry.

For the best trio of light Brahma 1.00
" dark " 1.00
" Plymouth Rock 1.00
" buff Cochin 1.00
" brown Leghorn 1.00
" white " 1.00
" black Spanish 1.00
" Partridge Cochin 1.00
" Ducks 1.00
" Pigeons 1.00
" Turkeys 1.00

A poster for the 1879 Fair and Cattle Show. The Farmers and Mechanics Club of Wilmington was organized in 1875 by Harrison Allen Sheldon, son of Asa G. Sheldon (1788–1870), and one of the premier annual events in town during that time was their Fair and Cattle Show. This poster lists the prizes for the best livestock and agricultural products the farmers of the town could produce.

An 1856 map of the area around the original Baldwin Apple tree. Discovered by Squire Samuel Thompson in 1793 while surveying for the Middlesex Canal, the Baldwin Apple has become a symbol of the town almost as familiar as the Whitefield Elm. Originally called the Butter, Woodpecker, or Pecker Apple, it got its current name from Colonel Loammi Baldwin of Woburn, who cultivated this variety extensively in the early 1800s.

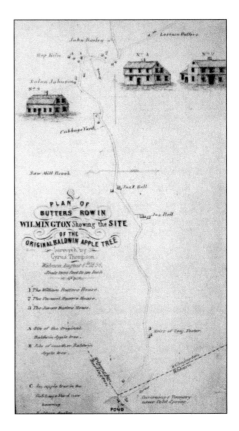

The Baldwin Monument. This stone pillar with a likeness of the Baldwin Apple on top was erected in 1895 by the Rumford Historical Association of Woburn to mark the site of the original tree, which was felled by a gale in 1815. The Baldwin Apple Monument, as it is now known, stands on Chestnut Street adjacent to the William Butters II House.

A scion of the original tree, probably planted by Colonel Baldwin or one of his sons in the early 1800s. This scion was most likely one on the trees indicated in the 1856 Plan of Butters Row shown on the previous page.

A *c.* 1900 photograph of Harrison Lincoln "Link" Sheldon with one of his cows. Link was an uncle to Wilbur Sheldon.

Harold Eames (left) and an unidentified man next to the Jaquith Hemlock, the largest hemlock tree in New England. The tree once stood on David Jaquith's property on Aldrich Road. Harold was the son of Ed Nelson Eames, a selectman and amateur photographer, who along with Arthur Thomas Bond took many photographs of the town around the turn of the century.

Abiel Carter's hop house on Glen Road near the crossing of the Lawrence Branch of the Boston and Lowell Railroad, c. 1898.

A photograph of what a typical barn around Wilmington looked like in the late 1890s. This particular structure still stands today behind the former Herbert Buck House on Middlesex Avenue in North Wilmington.

The Grange Hall on Wildwood Street, built in 1911. The Wilmington Grange was incorporated in 1907, and the Annual Grange Fair, like the Farmers and Mechanics Club Fair and Cattle Show, was a popular event for Wilmington farmers. The hall, which was used by many organizations and social clubs in town for parties, plays, and even basketball games, was destroyed by fire in 1970.

Cutting hay at the Brooks Farm on Burlington Avenue in the vicinity of present-day Dell Drive, c. 1913. From left to right are John Brooks, Paul Dayton, and William Brooks

Grandfather William Brooks haying in his fields. Despite its odd appearance, the reader can probably rest assured that the hat worn by Grandfather William Brooks kept the hot sun off of his head.

Paul Dayton and John Brooks after loading the hay. Unlike the modern machinery of today, which can cut or bale dozens of acres of hay in a day, small farms in town in the early 1900s relied on the strong arms and backs of their owners and helpers. Having cut their field by hand, Paul Dayton and John Brooks loaded the hay by pitchfork onto this horse-drawn wagon to be brought back to the barn for storage.

Leonard Chisholm's mink farm on Hopkins Street in the late 1940s. Although the mink farm and most of the mink houses are gone, the area is still worked as a small produce farm by Leonard's sons and grandsons. It is one of the few remaining farms in towns.

Eleven

People, Leisure, and Recreation

A memorial to Wilmington soldiers who fought and died in the Civil War. This monument is located in the Wildwood Cemetery and was erected by former Wilmington High School students in 1902. Many of the students responsible for the monument's creation had friends and classmates killed in the war.

Belinda Ward Clark (1815–1903), the second wife of Amasa Ford Clark of Danville, Vermont. Mrs. Clark was the mother of State Senator Chester Clark. For many years she lived in the large white house with attached barn that still stands on the corner of Middlesex Avenue and Clark Street.

Senator Chester Ward Clark (1851–1925). Senator Clark was educated at Phillips Academy in Exeter, New Hampshire, and he studied law in Boston. He was admitted to the Massachusetts Bar in 1878 and became a state representative and later a state senator.

Charles W. Swain (1826–1895), the son of Levi Swain. Charles Swain was the founder of the Wilmington Public Library. In 1871 he brought before the Annual Town Meeting an article which requested the formation of a public library. The article passed and later that year the library opened, with Swain serving as both librarian and treasurer.

An 1876 photograph of Rebecca Blanchard, *nee* Carter. She married Henry Blanchard, the son of William Blanchard Jr., in 1849. At the time the Blanchard's, one of the wealthiest families in town, lived in the Federal-style house at the corner of Glen Road adjacent to the Congregational church.

Thomas Davis Bond (1815–1888), the son of Joseph Bond Jr. Thomas Bond was one of the heirs to the Bond Cracker business. He built an opulent, Italianate Victorian-style house on Middlesex Avenue across from Adams Street in 1856 and lived there until his death. The house is now the property of the Archdiocese of Boston, serving as the rectory for St. Thomas of Villanova Church.

Olive Thompson (1822–1885). Olive Thompson married Thomas Davis Bond in 1845 and together they had five children including Lizzie Bond and Arthur Thomas Bond.

Arthur Thomas Bond (1852–1936), one of Captain Joseph Bond's great-grandsons. In 1898 Arthur Bond compiled a collection of Wilmington artifacts that he planned to use as the basis for a historical book on the town. When he was refused financial backing he moved from town taking his collection with him. Early in 1997 this collection was discovered and later sold to the town. Many photographs appearing in this book have come from that collection.

Lizzie Bond, the sister of Arthur Thomas Bond. Lizzie Bond was born in Wilmington in 1855 and on May 17, 1882, she married William Sweatt of Woonsocket, RI. This photograph shows her on her wedding day.

Susie Sheldon, *nee* Putnam, born in Wilmington in 1868. She was the second wife of Asa G. Sheldon (1862–1939) and the stepmother of Wilbur Sheldon.

Henry Sheldon and Sarah Sheldon, *nee* Gowing, *c.* 1890s. Henry (1822–1902) was the son of Asa G. Sheldon (1788–1870).

A family photograph of Abbie and Charles Sargent with their infant son Edmund. Abbie was a daughter of Horace Sheldon, sister to Town Librarian Anna Tolman Sheldon, and a niece of Henry Sheldon.

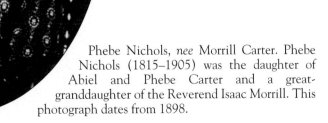

Phebe Nichols, *nee* Morrill Carter. Phebe Nichols (1815–1905) was the daughter of Abiel and Phebe Carter and a great-granddaughter of the Reverend Isaac Morrill. This photograph dates from 1898.

Mattie Eames, *nee* Nichols, the wife of Ed Nelson Eames and the mother of Harold Eames. This *c.* 1900 photograph was probably taken somewhere on Woburn Street (note the streetcar electric line in the background).

Harold Eames (right), an unidentified friend, and a dog navigating around a pond in Wilmington on what appears to be a less than seaworthy raft.

France B. Hiller (1845–1900). The eccentricities of Mrs. Hiller were well known to the townspeople during the late 1800s. She and her first husband made their fortune through cranberry growing and a pharmaceutical business. She was known as the "Casket Lady" for the elaborately carved wooden coffins she commissioned built for her and her first husband. She is said to have regularly slept in her casket, which was kept at her house.

Henry Hiller II (1869–1958), born Pierre Surrette in Ellsbrook, Nova Scotia. He was working as the Widow Hiller's coachman when he married her in 1893. Deeply devoted to her late husband and wanting to perpetuate his family name, she convinced Pierre to change his. She died in 1900, but mindful of her wishes Henry Hiller II kept his adopted name through life.

121

The first Wilmington High School basketball team. The new sport of basketball was still in its infancy when the first Wilmington High School team posed for this 1908 photograph. Pictured are, from left to right, as follows: (front row) Augustus McMahon, Joseph Strong, and Harold Eames; (back row) Principal Seth Loring, Harris Hemeon, Rodney Buck, and Eddie Neilson.

The Silver Lake baseball team. Behind the still legal spitball of ace pitcher Eddie Neilson (sitting, second from left), the Silver Lake baseball team defeated all comers for two straight years beginning c. 1908. Whether it was in front of their own crowded grandstand at the field off Cottage Street or when they traveled by trolley to away games, the team was unbeatable.

The Wilmington High School Baseball Team on the steps of the high school, c. 1915. Future Superintendent of Streets James White is pictured in the front row, third from the left, and future Postmaster Henry Porter is also in the front row, fifth from the left.

Two young ladies enjoying a tranquil canoe ride on the river while their male companions wait on shore, 1908. The Shawsheen River, a tributary of the Merrimack River, runs parallel to Hopkins and Lake Streets and forms the border with Billerica on the west side of town.

The International Order of Odd Fellows Whitefield Lodge, as the Wilmington chapter was known, in front of the grange hall on September 27, 1930. They turned out for this panoramic

dd Fellows, unit of Parade." September 27 1930.

photograph in full dress regalia in order to celebrate the bicentennial anniversary of Wilmington's incorporation as a town.

The drum and bugle corps of Wilmington's Post 136, c. 1930. Wilmington's Post 136 of the American Legion was founded in 1919 by World War I veteran Captain Joseph Strong. The organization originally met at the grange hall and then at the former Catholic Club Building on the corner of Middlesex Avenue and Adams Street.

Miss Eames, a teacher at the West School for many years, and her students on the town common in 1942. Judging from the dress this was probably a May Day celebration which children from all the town's schools participated in. The house that can be seen in the background stands across from the front entrance to Wilmington High School.

Attorney Philip Buzzell (1892–1978), the son of Dr. Daniel Buzzell. Philip Buzzell served as town counsel for over thirty-five years. In addition to his duties in town government, he was a devoted trustee of the Wilmington Public Library, a position he maintained from 1931 until the time of his death.

Olive Sheldon, *nee* Carter (1903–1973), the widow of Wilbur Sheldon. A familiar face in town government, she served on the board of assessors, on the WPA, as a ballot clerk, and as clerk of the board of selectmen.

The Wilmington Skating Club, located on an outdoor rink behind the South School on Chestnut Street. In the late 1950s and early 1960s speed skating was all the rage in town, especially when Jeanne Ashworth of Church Street became the first American woman to win a medal in Olympic speed skating competition. Jeanne won a bronze medal in the 500 meter event at the 1960 Winter Olympics in Squaw Valley, California.

Frank Willis Dayton (1874–1949). Frank Dayton was born in Manchester, New Hampshire, and moved to Wilmington in 1898. He was first elected selectman in 1930 and served as such until his death. In addition to his many years in town government, he was an employee of the Boston and Maine Railroad for fifty-six years. He is the father of Paul Dayton and the grandfather of Bill Dayton.